A 31-Day Devotional for Love & Justice

THE BOOK OF EL OVE

by
Joshua Nelson, DMin and Kimberly Nelson, PhD

The Book of EL
published by Watersprings Publishing, a division of
Watersprings Media House, LLC.
P.O. BOX 1284
Olive Branch, MS 38654
www.waterspringsmedia.com
Contact publisher for bulk orders and permission requests.

Copyrights © 2019 by Joshua and Kimberly Nelson
All rights reserved. No part of this publication may be reproduced, distributed, or transmitted in any form or by any means, including photocopying, recording, or other electronic or mechanical methods, without the prior written permission of the publisher, except in the case of brief quotations embodied in critical reviews and certain other noncommercial uses permitted by copyright law.

Printed in the United States of America.

Library of Congress Control Number: 2019917663

ISBN-13: 978-1-948877-38-1

Scripture quotations from THE MESSAGE. Copyright © by Eugene H. Peterson 1993, 1994, 1995, 1996, 2000, 2001, 2002. Used by permission of NavPress Publishing Group.

Scripture quotations credited to NASB are from the New American Standard Bible, copyright © 1960, 1962, 1963, 1968, 1971, 1972, 1973, 1975, by the Lockman Foundation. Used by permission.

Scripture quotations credited to NIV are from the Holy Bible, New International Version. Copyright © 1973, 1978, 1984, 2011 by Biblica, Inc. Used by permission. All rights reserved worldwide.

Scripture quotations marked "NKJV" are taken from the New King James Version. Copyright © 1982 by Thomas Nelson, Inc. Used by permission. All rights reserved.

Scripture quotations marked "NKJV" are taken from the New King James Version. Copyright © 1982 by Thomas Nelson, Inc. Used by permission. All rights reserved.

Scripture quotations marked (CEV) are from the Contemporary English Version ©1991, 1992, 1995 by American Bible Society. Used by Permission.

Table of Contents

	Introduction	i
	How To Read This Devotional	iii
Day 1	Made Flesh	1
Day 2	Transformed To Love	4
Day 3	Seek God, Seek Justice	7
Day 4	Buy A Bigger Pot	10
Day 5	Open Your Mouth	13
Day 6	Defenders	16
Day 7	Get Mad	19
Day 8	Anomaly	22
Day 9	Netflix And Justice	25
Day 10	Me The Innkeeper	28
Day 11	Real Christians, Please Stand Up	31
Day 12	God Of Justice	35
Day 13	Transforming Love	38
Day 14	The Social Justice Holiday	41
Day 15	The Slaying	44
Day 16	Deliver Us!	47
Day 17	Discovering The Hidden	50
Day 18	The Shout	53
Day 19	Division Vs. Unity	56
Day 20	God With US	59
Day 21	Privileged Perspectives	62
Day 22	On The Side Of Justice	66
Day 23	We In This Together	69
Day 24	Finding My Religion	72
Day 25	You Become What You Worship	75
Day 26	Tap Into The Power	78
Day 27	Spirit Action	81
Day 28	Golden Rule	85
Day 29	The Paradigm Shift	88
Day 30	Last Word	91
Day 31	To Know Him	94
Appendix	Exploring Ubuntu And Restorative Justice	97
	Charity Vs. Justice Spectrum	102
	Actions Of Love	103
	Social Justice Project Ideas	104
	Bibliography	105
	About The Authors	107

DEDICATED TO
the Least, the Last, and the Lost.

ACKNOWLEDGEMENTS

Our Family
Christopher Nelson, Sherri Nelson, Michele Nelson, Romeo Dawes, Maulet Dawes, and Antonet Dawes...

Thank you for your continued prayers
and support in everything we do.

INTRODUCTION

God demonstrated His love by giving. So, we learn that love is an action that gives. We discover in John 3:16 that love gives from its "only", from what belongs to it. Love is unconditional and sacrificial because it gives of itself despite the pain it will incur. God's love gives Himself to die on the cross for us. He pays the price that sin demands, He pays the price that was ours to pay. He had no obligation to save us, yet God sends Himself, Jesus Christ, the only begotten Son who dwells with us.

Since we are God's children, made in His image, we relate to Jesus as our Elder Brother. When we believe in Him, we become like Him. We begin to love like He loves. We begin to give like He gives. We begin to war against sin like He did. When we encounter the pain and injustice that sin brings to this world, our hearts knit with Gods, in desire for justice and restoration.

God's character towards seeking justice is clearly displayed throughout all pages of scripture. To know the gospel is to know justice. The goal of the gospel is to call sinners to repentance, to end oppression. Social justice within the gospel seeks to alleviate suffering with the primary goal of saving both the oppressed and the oppressor. This attention to both groups is where we gather the major principles for restorative justice. Restorative justice specifically reaches both the oppressor and oppressed in hopes to restore a better society.

The original problem for the Christian is sin, and sin leads to injustice. Thus, the goal becomes social or restorative justice in lieu of repentance and the hope of an earth made new in righteousness. Biblical justice is more restorative than man's punitive justice. While God does condemn and punish oppressors/sinners He does this after opportunities for repentance, and always for the purpose of ending more pain toward the oppressed.

The ultimate goal of justice activism for a Christian is the supreme rulership of Jesus Christ. This is why the three Angel's message in Revelation chapter 14 is so crucial. It speaks to the entrance of God's hour of judgment. The Bible makes it clear that Jesus is to judge the earth. Jesus is perfect righteousness and is the only one who can truly usher in justice on earth. As one seeks justice in the community, we seek Christ's will on earth as it is in heaven.

The Book of EL: Love

HOW TO READ THIS DEVOTIONAL

*E*ach devotional can be read at one time, or throughout the week. After each devotional there is a prayer. Before reading each devotional read the entire chapter and context of the focal verse to capture the full lesson. Pray and specifically ask God to cover you with the Holy Spirit to gain deeper understanding and wisdom. Use the space at the end of each devotional to record God's words to you, and what He is asking you to do differently. In the back of this book you will find additional readings on restorative justice. We are most excited about the "Love in Action" section where we give a plethora of ideas on how to implement actions of love and justice into your everyday life of ministry.

Why "el" L?

El – Hebrew name for God used over 200 times in the Old Testament, often combined with other descriptions of God.
El Elyon – The Most-High God (Gen 14:18)
El Olam - The God of eternity (Gen 21:33)
El Yeshuati – God of my Salvation (Isa 12:2)
Elohim – the living God (Gen 1:1)
Elohay Mishpat – God of Justice (Isa 30:18)
Elohay Mikarov - God who is near (Jer 23:23)
Elohay Tehilati – God of My Praise (Ps 109:1)
Elohay Selichot - God of Forgiveness (Neh 9:17)
Elohay Elohim – God of Gods (Deut 10:17)

L – Love, the greatest attribute of God (1 Cor 13)

L – the "L" community we have been called to love; least, last, lost, left out, looser, lonely (Matt 25)

DAY 1
MADE FLESH

MATTHEW 25:40 NKJV
And the King will answer and say to them, 'Assuredly, I say to you, inasmuch as you did it to one of the least of these My brethren, you did it to Me.'

Life's most important question is being answered right now as we live our lives. God is asking us 'what are you doing to the least, the last, and the lost?' I was first introduced to this question as a doctoral student visiting thriving churches in Chicago, Illinois. The church that I visited amazed me at their ability to authentically live the great commission. They were obedient to the word of God in doctrine and deed, because for them, truth was simply a better view of love. The more truth we have the more love we should show. They lived out their doctrine in how they treated those in their community. Being a church meant becoming the walking, breathing reality of the kingdom of God. They were the extension of Immanuel, the Word made flesh, the incarnation sent to their community. God was with their community because they were with their community. In that neighborhood in Chicago, God was more than a Word, He had a face, hands, and feet...He was made flesh.

God is looking for men and women to fully surrender to His Spirit and receive the mind of Christ. The mind of Christ repeats God's pressing theme; to seek and save the lost. The process of Salvation transforms a sinner to a believer and a believer to a disciple. A disciple is one that follows the leader so much that their actions inadvertently become identical. When someone knows me, they should begin to know God.

Today's Prayer

Lord, help me to answer the question of what I am doing to help the least, the last, and the lost. Help me to be obedient to Your word so much so that it becomes flesh through me. Lord reveal to me what blocks me from helping others, and use me even as I am trying to remove the blocks. Help me Lord to be a change agent within my community. Reveal the work You want me to do and help me to be open to whatever You want of me. I want to be able to fully surrender to You. I understand it is a process so lead me through the process so I can lead others in their process. Thank You for hearing and answering this prayer.
Amen.

The Book of EL: Love

My Reflections

DAY 2

TRANSFORMED TO LOVE

MATTHEW 25:37 KJV
Then the righteous will answer Him saying, 'Lord, when did we see You hungry and feed You, or thirsty and give You drink?

One day God will separate those dedicated to service (the sheep) from those consumed with self (the goats) vs. 32. The sheep do not even know they are doing anything special as they ask, "When did we see You...?" The proof they have been saved by grace is in how grace has transformed their daily actions. The core of grace is natural love. It is when we become so filled with His love that we naturally begin to reach out to those who are considered the marginalized and downtrodden in this life. This is what love does, love champions the looser. For God so loved us that He decided to give all of heaven in the person of Jesus Christ to sinners destined to die unless they believed in the Son.

When we serve the L community, we serve El Yeshuati. We may be afraid about ministering to the undesirables of this life, but how can we fear our Lord? The closer we become to people who desperately need love is when we come closer to our Lord. The closer we come to our Lord, the more we realize that we should have been considered undesirable and undeserving.

The sheep ask the question because it has become a part of their lives of grace to serve others. In our Christian life we often concern ourselves too much with our deficiencies instead of just receiving God's mercies. God is the one in us giving us the power and will to do good deeds to those around us. When we feel distant from Him, we can always find Him in the eyes of one of the L's.

Service always blesses at least two, us and the one we serve. When we stop navel gazing and look forward into His wonderful face, we see the purpose of life. It is not about our troubles but about His strength. In our most painful hours, we have been trained to look for His hand and trust in His heart of love. Our perspective changes from our woes and focuses on how He is using us for His glory. Ultimately God is trying to input His love in His creatures to spread it to the world. This plan must be quickly fulfilled so that we can receive the Kingdom at the second coming. God saves us to save others.

Today's Prayer

Lord, I give You thanks for saving me. Thank You for teaching me that there is more to my life than just my needs. You saved me to save others. Lord, I ask that You place me in situations to serve others. Even when I am focusing on myself, place me in situations to focus on the people around me who are also in need. I understand now that when I help others, I am also helping myself. Evoke the power You placed in me to serve, and to draw closer to You.
Amen.

My Reflections

DAY 3
SEEK GOD, SEEK JUSTICE

Isaiah 1:17 NIV
*Learn to do right; seek justice.
Defend the oppressed.
Take up the cause of the fatherless;
plead the case of the widow.*

After church one Sabbath, some church members were talking amongst themselves and sharing their disgust with the supposed "thugs" who hung out on the corner near the church. They were disturbed that they had to drive past this dilapidated house on their way to church. They saw no connection between their worship at church and their imperative to seek justice. Those who had been recipients of a racist and screwed up system were now being labeled and ostracized by these Christians. I could not help but feel saddened by the juxtaposition. These faithful church goers had been praying and worshiping God for years unaware that their mindsets were causing a blockade between them and God. I decided to use the moment to teach, and so I encouraged them to go and talk with the young men. I pleaded that we had a responsibility to minister to those in need, even if that meant we showed up late for church. How could we drive past these houses filled with people desperately needing the love of God only to rush to a building to sing about love we failed to demonstrate? That day I had to practice what I had preached. I went over to the young men and learned that their mother had actually been a member of the church at some point. The boys had been raised Christians. We sat and talked about God for almost an hour. I wish I could tell you that the boys gave their lives back to God. However, their mother did begin to study with our church and a few months after was rebaptized into the church.

We can say we love God, but our love is demonstrated, not only proclaimed. The world learns about God's love through those who proclaim to know and serve Him. Since we are born into sin, it is easy to be drawn towards wrong and injustice. Many people are self-absorbed, but Isaiah's message from God calls for us to consider others. In fact, the verbs used in this text are of the imperative, which highlights the intensity of the expectations. We are then expected to defend, take up the cause of, and plead the case of those being treated unfairly. This may not be innate but as we fall deeper in love with Jesus, we fall deeper in love with people. His Holy Spirit teaches us how to love justly.

Today's Prayer

Father as I fall in love with You, help me to fall in love with the people around me. Help me to demonstrate and not just proclaim my love for You through how I treat and care for others. Help me to die to self daily, where I am weak, make me strong. Let the needs of others be ever in the forefront of my mind. Amen.

My Reflections

DAY 4

BUY A BIGGER POT

Zechariah 7:9-10 NIV
"This is what the Lord Almighty said: 'Administer true justice; show mercy and compassion to one another. Do not oppress the widow or the fatherless, the foreigner or the poor. Do not plot evil against each other.

Have you ever stopped and asked yourself "why"? Why do you do the things you do? Why do you engage in certain habits or behaviors? There is a story I once heard about a woman who taught her daughter to always cut the heads off of the fish before putting it in the pot. One day the daughter asked her mom why she did that since she would cook the fish heads separate. Her mother thought for a moment and shrugged, saying, "I'm not sure I just know my mother always did it." Thankfully the girl's grandmother was sitting in the other room. The girl asked grandma who looked up over her glasses smiling and said, "Hunny I just didn't have a big enough pot, cutting off the heads was the only way the fish would fit." Sometimes we glorify pointless practices that are purely based on tradition. Everything we do can eventually fade from its original significance and meaning.

In the text the people had fasted and mourned on this special day for so long they just kept doing it because that was what they always did. They began to engage in their tradition for themselves and not for God. So many times, we continue in some methodology because of nostalgia or habit. We think by engaging in an activity we did when we were spiritually connected, the act will keep us spiritually connected. God is angry at this type of thinking because it centers the worshipper back towards themselves. God challenges their religion by how they are treating other people. If we are going to truly please God, our focus must shift from dead rituals for ourselves toward behaviors that restore the less fortunate.

The sad part about this passage continues as the people refuse to listen to God. In fact, they shrug their shoulders, plug their ears, and allow their hearts to become set in their ways. This type of disobedience is cultivated over time. The scariest part is that people in this state may actually think they are doing the right thing because they are engaging in religious traditions, but once these practices lose their meaning and connection to the worshipper's heart, they become useless. We must be willing to examine our rituals and be brave enough to buy a bigger pot when needed. We need to center our minds on the main thing, which is getting to know the heart of God. What are the areas in your life where you feel God challenging you to change? How can we avoid our hearts becoming hard over time? How can we remain open to reaching out to our fellow man?

Today's Prayer

Lord I plead with You to pull me from tradition if it is getting in the way of our relationship. Open my eyes to the things I am doing that keep me away from You, and possibly hurting others. Pull me out of useless repetition and give me insight in what it is You want of me. Align my heart and mind with Yours daily.
Amen.

My Reflections

The Book of EL: Love

DAY 5

OPEN YOUR MOUTH

Proverbs 31:8-9 NASB
*Open your mouth for the mute,
For the rights of all the unfortunate.*

*Open your mouth, judge righteously,
And defend the rights of the afflicted and needy.*

We named our son Jude King, and oh how he has embraced his middle name. Even before turning one, our little man seemed to carry himself in a kingly way. We always laugh when we see how much our son behaves like we are his subjects. Most parents want their children to grow up believing they are special and important just like a King. But what we don't want, is for our children to grow up entitled. It seems this is the fear of King Lemuel's mother in the text. She cautions her son against drinking because she knows it will cloud his judgment and lead towards mistreating the poor. It strikes me how important this was for her. Is this a pressing concern for you in your life and your family? Each one of us are the royalty of God, which gives us the same responsibility as a king, to defend and open our mouths for the less fortunate. How can we live royal lives that look out for the L community? Not only should we open our mouths for the poor, but this speaks to how we should give them back their voice. How can we give a voice to the voiceless in our community? We often think people can simply try harder to pull themselves out of their situations. People who think this way often don't understand the psychology of poverty or systematic oppression. Those of us that have privileges, and are blessed with certain access have a responsibility to ensure the voiceless are heard. This may mean highlighting stories from residents with extremely high light bills, visiting with veterans, or even advocating for immigrants and refugees.

Today's Prayer

*Father direct me today to stand and open my mouth for those who do not have a voice. I do not know where to start but I am opening myself up to You to show me. Give me the courage, the words, and knowledge to be an advocate today. Bring people into my life who can teach me if needed, and allow me to stand firm on Your promises that You will lead me where I need to go.
Amen.*

My Reflections

DAY 6
DEFENDERS

JEREMIAH 22:3 NASB
Thus says the Lord, "Do justice and righteousness, and deliver the one who has been robbed from the power of his oppressor. Also do not mistreat or do violence to the stranger, the orphan, or the widow; and do not shed innocent blood in this place.

*J*eremiah was willing to deliver this strong and crucial message directly to the King in the land. God wanted to remind the leader of his responsibility in protecting the most vulnerable of society; immigrants, orphans, and widows. These three are still the most mistreated today. In America and other countries, immigration has become a controversial topic as many whites fear the browning of their country. Muslims and Mexicans are often the ones mistreated here in America. Orphans are being caused by corrupt politicians who separate Mexican families at the southern border. Many other children are being sold into sex slavery, sometimes these children are sold by their own relatives. Widows are made through the decisions of a few powerful and corrupt politicians who use sons and daughters as pawns in their violent wars. One parent is expected to carry the household alone while wars, domestic or abroad take the lives of their spouses. We see how the 1971 war on drugs contributed in removing Black husbands and fathers from the home totally dismantling the black family and future. This systematic widowing of black females has done untold damage to a nation.

Today we are inundated with stories of injustice oppressing the most vulnerable, while leaders in king-like positions stand idly by. In the text, the rewards for leaders protecting the rights of the oppressed are great.

The leader stands to gain what most leaders strive for anyways; respect and influence. But the consequences for disobeying God's justice plea is quite severe. In verse five God gives a strong, "I swear to Myself", that those who mistreat the least of these will be punished. In fact, the context reminds us of the covenant obligations found in Exodus 21:21-27, so crucial to securing the royal lineage which would lead to the messiah, Jesus Christ. If the king is negligent in defending the vulnerable in the society, God will be negligent in defending his legacy. We too often think that we gain more for ourselves when we focus on ourselves. The reality is that we gain more from God when our focus turns towards others. If you stand in power over anyone, as a boss, parent, civic leader, you have a responsibility to defend the vulnerable, not exploit.

Today's Prayer

Lord, today I'm asking that You open my heart and my eyes to the mistreatment of the least of these. At times I get caught up in my own world that I miss opportunities to help someone else, so I ask that You do not allow me to stand idly by as others suffer. I ask that You help me see outside of myself, and my family and try to do something today that will make a difference.
Amen.

My Reflections

DAY 7

GET MAD

Jeremiah 22:5 KJV
But if ye will not hear these words, I swear by myself, saith the Lord, that this house shall become a desolation.

Get mad! When we are angry at the action of injustice, we are connecting with the heart of God. We learn to "be angry and sin not" as we are filled with righteous indignation. Being complacent in the face of injustice is being complicit with the wrongs in your community. Too many of us dismiss inequities because they do not seem to directly affect us. We are lost in our own world aloof to the suffering of those on the other side of the tracks. We think that what we don't know won't hurt us. We are lost in lala land fighting over rubbish while people are dying, unjust laws are passed, and our own liberties are being removed. I have sat in too many church meetings that entertain pointless conversations that do nothing to deal with real life issues of people in the pews and neighborhood. I've seen too many people whose conversation is always about self. When we fail to observe our world through the lenses of Christ, we miss opportunities. We love to hide behind the walls of the church, our homes, careers, or relationships instead of opening our eyes to the world around us. Jesus needs your talents, your gifts to do your part in weaving the fabric of love this world desperately craves. Too often the world's problems seem too big and we opt to focus on our own comfort and self-interest. These pursuits are often entangled with the devil's plan to keep us from engaging in the war against sin and keep us from fulfilling our purpose. We must learn to get angry. Anger is not always bad. God has given us this emotion for good. We often use it for our own desires, revenge and outbursts, but if we lean into the emotion of anger, we will begin to hate what God hates. We will begin to love what God loves. We will burn with passion to move into action and transform His world. Righteous anger fuels the engine of God's justice reformation. So, reflect for a minute and allow the Spirit to consume your desires. Where is the Holy Spirit leading you? What disturbs you? What is He asking you to help change? Allow His anger to fuel your life's purpose.

Today's Prayer

My Father, You do not like what is happening to Your people, especially those who cannot help themselves. Help me to develop a distaste for wrong doing, mistreatment, and be moved to do something to help someone who is being taken advantage of this week. Help me keep an eye out for those who are unable to help themselves. Provide me with the resources needed to help in whatever capacity, in Your name Father.
Amen.

My Reflections

DAY 8

ANOMALY

ROMANS 12:15-18 NASB
Take care of God's needy people and welcome strangers into your home. Ask God to bless everyone who mistreats you. Ask him to bless them and not to curse them. When others are happy, be happy with them, and when they are sad, be sad. Be friendly with everyone. Don't be proud and feel that you are smarter than others. Make friends with ordinary people. Don't mistreat someone who has mistreated you. But try to earn the respect of others and do your best to live at peace with everyone.

We have a responsibility to live as Christians. Becoming a Christian is not a solitary journey to heaven, we travel together. In fact, the life of a Christian is abnormal, counter-cultural and unorthodox. Most good people would see the decency of treating those in need with kindness. However, Paul is speaking about more than just rolling down one's window and giving a dollar at the traffic light. In the Greek the phrase in verse 15 is "given to hospitality" which is an interesting idea. Hospitality actually means to "welcome strangers" while the word "given" often means "persecute". So, the idea is that we love with intense action those who we do not even know. We learn to integrate persistent love into the life of strangers in need. Not only that, but the text says we must even bless the ones who cuss us out or mean us harm. This is abnormal, to be a Christian is to be supernatural, to watch God perform miracles in your behavior. When someone in need interacts with us, they should experience miracles. We should not be affected by the negativity of the world, but we should infect the world with the miracle of peace. In a world of injustice, we need peace. Wherever we go we should be conduits of peace. This peace is an anomaly today, but it is what the world needs now. When there is no justice, there is no peace. But where there is peace, there is justice.

Today's Prayer

Lord, at times I live in isolation not realizing the needs of others. Help me to be a source of encouragement, strength, and support to those who are on this life journey. If in any way I contribute to isolating others, please point it out to me and give me the opportunity to invite others into Your circle. Those who have isolated me in some way or cursed me, I ask that You bless them, and I lift them now to You.
Amen.

My Reflections

DAY 9
NETFLIX AND JUSTICE

MICAH 6:8 NASB
*He has told you, O man, what is good;
And what does the Lord require of you
But to do justice, to love kindness,
And to walk humbly with your God?*

*I*n the last days the Bible speaks about people who will be consumed by their own desires and knowledge. Every day I see this displayed in how certain so many are in what they believe. For many they believe what feels right to them or what can be proved logically. Too many are being deceived because they have no idea what is right, or what God really wants. Preachers, teachers, leaders, politicians, and experts all claim they know the way. So many beliefs, ideologies, and doctrines but those teachings must be centered on what God requires. Religious people can require so much from the behavior of its followers. The Spirit of God is concerned with personal piety and relational responsibility. The requirement is to make sure that justice is done and that our first concern is kindness. This means that we cannot live our lives ignoring the injustice around us. Our responsibility is to see that justice is done. Our vital concern is not our 401K or preserving our way of life, instead our duty is to be mindful of the people around us. This way of thinking can only happen when we learn to walk in humility with God. In fact, how else can we walk with God, but humbly. We must ask ourselves if our first impulse is not to seek justice or kindness, then are we truly walking with God?

My life is often consumed with so much busy work. When I first get up in the morning it is easy to reach for my phone before reaching for God. I can easily go through a day and never consider my fellow man. My free time is often spent watching Netflix, scrolling through my social media, or texting friends. Everywhere I turn, someone or something is requiring my time and attention. It's not very difficult to squeeze God and His mission out of my life. While I desperately want to be successful in life, I often forget the most important task. What should be primary in our lives is centering our time on fulfilling the Lord's requirements. How can you walk humbly with God? How will you do justice? What does it mean to love kindness?

Today's Prayer

Lord, I ask that You create in me an urgency to be concerned about the people around me. Give me a heart that extends beyond myself and towards the injustices that hinder the progress of those who are down and out. Clear my own troubles so I can make time to help and focus on others.
Amen.

The Book of EL: Love

My Reflections

DAY 10
ME THE INNKEEPER

LUKE 10:36-37 NASB
"Which of these three do you think proved to be a neighbor to the man who fell into the robbers' hands?" And he said, "The one who showed mercy toward him." Then Jesus said to him, "Go and do the same."

While this famous parable is certainly focused on the kindness of the Samaritan to his would-be Jewish enemy, we must not forget the innkeeper. Remember the theme for this parable is mercy and how those seeking eternal rewards achieve this not by keeping the letter of the law but instead by living it. Jesus is teaching that one must be naturally able to show unbiased mercy to strangers. Jesus is the one who shows us how to see people in their distress. He puts in us a love that makes it impossible to ignore suffering. He gives us the desire and wisdom on how to act for the health and benefit of the needy. As we care for those cast to the roadside by poverty, sickness, incarceration, racism, violence, we are joining with Jesus. We are pouring the oil of His Spirit to sooth the pain and offering the wine of His blood to heal the soul. But like the Samaritan, Christ has left to prepare a place for us. He has left the needy at the inn and we are the innkeeper. Think about it. I have seen too many evangelistic events where the focus is on how many people are baptized and saved but not so much on healing and long-term transformation. The church has a responsibility to care for people who are brought to the inn. The saving and baptizing are reserved for the Holy Spirit.

When I married my wife, the focus was on the marriage not the wedding. Wait let me rethink that,

Kimberly definitely made sure the wedding was a focal highlight. But while we spent probably way too much money on just a few hours of celebration...we both know that the wedding was a gateway to the more important lifetime of marriage. Many marriages do fail because of a lack of endurance. There are rough patches where you feel like giving up. But we remember we made a choice, a decision for God, a responsibility to be true to each other. As people in relationship with Jesus we have the great responsibility of caring for others who have been brought to the inn. The work of discipling, restoring, or rehabilitating doesn't happen in one day, but healing takes place over time at the inn. We must show more than moments of charity but a lifestyle of justice and mercy to our fellowman. In your life today who is in your inn? Who has God placed in your life for you to care for and heal? It may be tempting to give up or pass by, but I challenge you to endure. God will be back soon, and we must be found working for His children.

Today's Prayer

Lord, this week I want to give unbiased mercy to strangers around me. Help me not to pass judgement, or to look down on others, but instead take action for the benefit of not myself, but to benefit those who are in need. Allow me to make time to spend pouring into the lives of others. Place me in situations where I can be a healing place for someone, rather than just a brief moment of relief.
Amen.

My Reflections

DAY 11

REAL CHRISTIANS, PLEASE STAND UP

Matt 7:12 NASB
"In everything, therefore, treat people the same way you want them to treat you, for this is the Law and the Prophets.

Jesus reminds us that the Bible He read from (the law and the prophets) was all about treating others with kindness. In John 5:39 Jesus tells a bunch of religious fanatics that they have read the Bible but have missed out on the true subject; Himself. When we desire to be like Jesus, we desire to treat people in a kind and just manner. When we study the Bible to find truth, we are actually studying to discover how to treat people. When we read the scriptures and learn how to behave, we are behaving so we can treat people how Jesus treats people.

I have never understood the common encounter with cantankerous religious persons, this should be an oxymoron. To be a student of the Bible should directly result in how we treat those around us. Christians should be the most loving and caring people in the world. It is sad today that many see evangelicals and other Christians as rude and vile. Those claiming to be Christians too often use or blindly support those who use derogatory language, ignorant stereotypes, and racist epitaphs. Some of the most hurtful experiences in my life happened through the efforts of religious people.

When a Christian behaves cruelly or insensitively, it makes them unworthy to carry that name. I would much rather we not even refer to them as Christians. A while back a young man from Florida was arrested after he posed as a medical doctor. Calling himself a doctor made no difference because professionally he did not possess the proper training or degree to use that title. To be considered a Christian we must be like Christ.

Jesus reminds us that "in everything" to treat people as we would want to be treated. Think for a moment about how most of us want to be treated. We desire respect, compassion, and sincerity. We crave comfort, security, and peace. We cherish freedom, liberty, and justice. We deserve access to healthcare, quality education, and equitable housing conditions. We expect equal protection under the law, unbiased treatment, and equal access to labor. If these are the values we want and expect, then others should also receive them. But there are too many who are not afforded these privileges. We often treat people differently based on their color, sex, age, status, or orientation. When we say we are treating the less fortunate in our community the way we want to be treated we fool ourselves. How can we drive past ghettos, hospitals, and prisons filled with people we know are victims of a flawed system and not speak out against the inequalities? How are we able to sleep easy knowing our church or our influence is doing nothing to make changes to the lives of those suffering? Those privileged in America experience an unnatural amount of ease and comfort while millions around us suffer untold terror and pain. In our complacency we are allowing mistreatment to continue in ways we would never allow ourselves to be treated.

Today's Prayer

Lord, as I continue to be a follower of You and dig into Your word, please let the word take over my spirit to be used for Your will. Unfold in Your word how I should treat others and meet the requirements of what it is to be a Christian. As I follow You, help those around me to see Your kindness and Your unconditional love. Please reveal Yourself through me as I interact with all people.
Amen.

My Reflections

DAY 12
GOD OF JUSTICE

AMOS 5:14-15 NASB
*Seek good and not evil, that you may live;
And thus may the Lord God of hosts be with you,
Just as you have said!*

*Hate evil, love good,
And establish justice in the gate!
Perhaps the Lord God of hosts
May be gracious to the remnant of Joseph.*

We may think that God doesn't see the injustice happening in the nation today. We may think He sees but just does not care. Or maybe He sees and cares but is unable to change it. Through the prophet Amos we discover that God sees all the dirt the nation does in the dark. He also calls out their hypocrisy as they claim to the world, they are God's servants but continue to practice injustice. The way in which God solves the injustice problem right now is through the miraculous power, wisdom, and courage He puts inside of us His followers. His message is simple to those who are doing or allowing injustice; "hate evil, love good". Good versus evil, the great controversy is the war that tips the tide of justice in our nation. If we love good, we will build up justice at the gate. The gate is the entrance of the city, the place where court was held, and the fate of criminals was decided. This means that we must uphold justice at the beginning of everything in the city. All that enters into society must be filtered through the gate of justice. Leaders and politicians have a responsibility to do justice. Christians know justice because they know God. When we fail to speak truth to power, we are depriving our communities of God's justice imperative. Who else can truly have a pulse for justice in our cities but the faith-based community? Justice should be best explained by the people in our communities claiming to be closest to the One who is just.

Today's Prayer

Father develop in me a hate for evil and a love for good. Point out the good in all people so I can treat them how You treat me. Even in my filth, You look upon me and pour out Yourself to me, Lord help me do the same for those who are deserving and undeserving. Though hard, help show me this week how to pour out myself to my brothers and sisters. Amen.

My Reflections

DAY 13
TRANSFORMING LOVE

1 John 3:17-18 NASB
But whoever has the world's goods, and sees his brother in need and closes his heart against him, how does the love of God abide in him? Little children, let us not love with word or with tongue, but in deed and truth.

Many of us would say we don't have the world's goods. We are trying to just get by ourselves. It really isn't in our budget to help every poor person we see. While I strongly believe in the literal lesson of this passage that requires the rich to distribute their goods to the poor, I also think there is a larger spiritual principle we must discover. What hopefully stands out to us is the issue of "closing our hearts" to those in need. Opening one's heart does not always require the donation of money or the distribution of goods. The needs of God's people are vast and changing. To have the love of God within us means our heart is open to discovering these intricate needs. This discovery is based in love that is exercised through action and truth. Action is greater than activity because activity is for the moment and action is for lasting change. Truth is greater than awareness for awareness can be surface, but truth is an expansive understanding. When we see the homeless, poor, prisoner, or even those who are abusers and criminals our hearts can open to a love rooted in action and truth. Nothing happens in a vacuum and people make choices for various reasons, but our heart opens to everyone with needs because we know the transforming power of the love that abides in us. We realize that love is more valuable than our goods. By opening up our hearts to those in need we began a transformation in their lives with the most transformative power in the universe; love.

Today's Prayer

Lord continue to open my heart not only through financial donations, but in the sacrifice of my time, energy, and mental capabilities. Help me to discover the intricate needs of others and be moved to action. Lord, I do not want to be hesitant but willingly urgent in my pursuit to do justice daily. Reveal to me the true nature of Justice and allow me to embrace it wholeheartedly.
Amen.

My Reflections

DAY 14
THE SOCIAL JUSTICE HOLIDAY

Isaiah 58:6-12 NASB
*"Is this not the fast which I choose,
To loosen the bonds of wickedness,
To undo the bands of the yoke,
And to let the oppressed go free
And break every yoke?
"Is it not to divide your bread with the hungry
And bring the homeless poor into the house;
When you see the naked, to cover him;
And not to hide yourself from your own flesh?
"Then your light will break out like the dawn,
And your recovery will speedily spring forth;
And your righteousness will go before you;
The glory of the Lord will be your rear guard.*

Growing up a Seventh-day Adventist Christian we often quoted Isaiah 58:13-14 outside the context of the entire chapter. We were taught to highlight the "no pleasure" stipulation for the Sabbath day. This was a great proof passage for legalists to ensure Saturday and fun never comingled. Some went as far to even say "sex" was forbidden on the Sabbath since it involves pleasure. C'mon man! I never knew how ridiculous such an interpretation was until actually reading the entire chapter. One will easily learn that the pleasure in which God's Sabbath was supposed to deter was far worse than going to the beach or playing sports on the Sabbath. Isaiah 58:3 describes people finding pleasure in mistreating people. The insane posture of these people is that they are mistreating people and wondering why God is far from them. How naive to be so aloof to what truly concerns the heart of God. Our personal piety is meaningless without public pity to those God loves. It is when we learn to love like God that our light begins to burst forth. When we truly respect the Sabbath, we begin to do and say what God wants. The Sabbath should be the social justice day of the week. A weekly reminder of our responsibility to rest from doing our own pleasure which often leads to injustice. Instead we rest on the day God created nothing but time, time for the created to reflect on the will of the Creator. The will of the Creator is that we show love to His creatures. Imagine if everyone reserved the seventh-day as the Holiday that reminds us of our duty to God and our fellow man. God did tell us to remember, we too often have forgotten what we are remembering. Deuteronomy 5 says we are remembering God's power to deliver us from bondage. The Sabbath is also a day to praise God for His creative and recreative power. The Sabbath is full of social justice implications and reminders. Have you considered the spiritual and biblical implications of worshiping God on His day for justice?

Today's Prayer

As I continue to embrace the true nature of a social justice sabbath, Lord I pray that You will keep me busy doing Your will on the sabbath day, and each day of my life. Help me to reflect on what the sabbath really is about and give me opportunities to fulfill it. Let me experience the true nature of the sabbath by being with Your people and serving the least, lost, and the last.
Amen.

My Reflections

DAY 15
THE SLAYING

LUKE 4:17-20 NASB
*And He came to Nazareth, where He had been brought up; and as was His custom, He entered the synagogue on the Sabbath, and stood up to read. And the book of the prophet Isaiah was handed to Him. And He opened the book and found the place where it was written,
"The Spirit of the Lord is upon Me,
Because He anointed Me to preach the gospel to the poor.
He has sent Me to proclaim release to the captives,
And recovery of sight to the blind,
To set free those who are oppressed,
To proclaim the favorable year of the Lord."
And He closed the book, gave it back to the attendant and sat down; and the eyes of all in the synagogue were fixed on Him.*

I will never forget an experience during the first few years of my pastoral ministry where a friend invited me to her church's evening service. As I entered the church, I immediately noticed that no one greeted me or even looked my way. The service went on through the night and grew progressively louder and expressive. Women were falling on the floor as deaconess' covered the ladies' legs with white sheets. Men were shouting and running laps around the sanctuary. Children danced in the aisles. The ministers were prophesying, speaking in tongues, and anointing people with oil. I have since been in many similar worship environments that caused me to feel nothing like I did that evening.

I sat there so uncomfortable and desperate to leave. I remember looking back at the doors to strategize my exit only to see ushers standing poised with no emotion as if standing guard. It was the most terrifying experience because I knew the Spirit of God had not fallen on anyone in that room, yet something had caught hold of them.

The greatest evidence of this was not based on my own discomfort with another worship style or culture, no it was based on this verse and others like it in scripture.

Jesus quotes Isaiah in explaining the evidence that the Spirit of the Lord was upon Him. The Spirit fills and possesses individuals for a purpose beyond their own but often as a witness to the power of God. The Spirit of God uses us to preach the gospel to the poor, to proclaim release to the captives, and to give sight to the blind. And as I left that small country church late that evening, I noticed that those who had claimed to be filled with the Spirit said nothing to me, got back into their cars and continued with their lives as usual. Nothing had notably changed.

I believe we need nights where the entire place is shaken and people are slain in the Spirit, because it should lead to action. When the Spirit truly catches hold of us, the evidence will be seen in how we respond and begin to treat the least of those around us.

Today's Prayer

Father, I continue to pray for the Spirit to fall fresh on me daily. As I receive the Spirit, give me the confidence and power to preach the gospel, proclaim and heal those in need.
I invite you to use me Lord like never before to reach those who are in need of You.
I surrender my all to You today.
Amen.

My Reflections

DAY 16

DELIVER US!

Luke 4:17-20 NASB
And He came to Nazareth, where He had been brought up; and as was His custom, He entered the synagogue on the Sabbath, and stood up to read. And the book of the prophet Isaiah was handed to Him. And He opened the book and found the place where it was written,

*"The Spirit of the Lord is upon Me,
Because He anointed Me to preach the gospel to the poor.
He has sent Me to proclaim release to the captives,
And recovery of sight to the blind,
To set free those who are oppressed,
To proclaim the favorable year of the Lord."
And He closed the book, gave it back to the attendant and sat down; and the eyes of all in the synagogue were fixed on Him.*

How significant of Jesus to read this passage on the Sabbath day, the very day where justice and mercy were emphasized. It is on this day He decides to remind a group of legalists the real reason behind worship and His coming. His homecoming sermon was brief but powerful. It shakes us to the core because it cuts past our pomp and elaborate programming. His message reminds us what His focus was and what our focus should be. Since Jesus has come, we have access to this power, this anointing that proclaims a favorable year of our Lord. This referenced the Old Testament year of jubilee where justice was given; debts were cancelled, slaves set free, and restoration was instituted. Is this not the hope we want for our community? This is the message that will change the world for good. It is not a message stripped of its practical value for people's lives. A message not simply obsessed with saving the soul for the hereafter but a message with concern for life here and now. For as we call out against the oppression of the least of these, we also call out the oppressors. Our cry against injustice is also a cry against sin. Our proclamation is for the restoration and redemption of both those oppressed and the ones oppressing to come to Jesus for repentance. Sin impoverishes but Jesus makes us rich. Sin breaks hearts, but Jesus mends them. Sin makes people captive and enslave others, but Jesus sets us free. Sin blinds us but Jesus gives us sight and vision. The good news is that Jesus did not just come to only preach a good message of deliverance, He came to deliver us!

Today's Prayer

Today Lord, I cry out on behalf of the oppressed. I ask that You release those who are bound. Give them rest from the hard labor placed upon them by their oppressors. Place people in the lives of those in need to provide relief financially, emotionally, mentally, and physically. I call upon You Lord to remove obstacles and prepare a way out for everyone who is oppressed. Direct my path to someone this week I can use my time to help and provide some relief for.
Amen.

My Reflections

DAY 17
DISCOVERING THE HIDDEN

LUKE 4:17-20 CEV
Jesus closed the book, then handed it back to the man in charge and sat down. Everyone in the meeting place looked straight at Jesus.

Jesus left the Devil in the wilderness after forty days of temptation only to come home and find the Devil in the pews. His own neighbors and friends tried to murder Him on the Sabbath day after preaching a mighty sermon. Often the ones closest to us give us the least respect. In Christ's case these people wanted Him to prove His Godship by performing a miracle. Jesus exposes a major spiritual problem within these church people and their ancestors. It's one thing to call them out, but Jesus goes on and calls out their moms and pops.

He basically says that those foreigners and immigrants are more worthy of receiving a miracle than 4th generation Christians. Many of our churches are not experiencing the miracles of God while sinners in the community are receiving fresh sources of power. We discover that God's miracles of grace respond to faith not pedigree. Jesus does not hold back as to avoid hurting their feelings. Instead Jesus speaks truth that exposes the spiritual deprivation and racism within these proposed religious people. They got angry because Jesus told them something was wrong with them. They held a deep-seated bias against gentiles, the very ones God meant for them to reach. The people had such deep seeded national, religious, and political views that even when the Son of God tells them they are wrong they refuse to listen. This story teaches us at least two major points. First, we must be honest about our own biases. Often in our attempts to remain sanitized from the world we shrink from our Christian responsibilities and encase ourselves with bubbles of self-righteousness. We become entitled, arrogant, and blind for our own interests. Second, we must be willing to call out such behavior in ourselves and others at the expense of harsh retaliation. I mean seriously, they tried to murder Jesus because He told them the truth about themselves. How hard is it for us to respond to the conviction of the Spirit? What deep seated truths have you held that need to be challenged? How do you determine what is right or wrong? Who ultimately decides what you believe?

Today's Prayer

As I go through today, Lord give me the strength to be honest about my own biases and judgements I may have about others. Let me look internally daily to admonish the things that are not of You. Lord give me the will-power to call out behavior that is unlike You in myself first, and in those who I hold dear. Give me the words to say and the heart of love to demonstrate Your love. Challenge me today Lord and help me meet the challenge each day I draw closer to You. Amen.

My Reflections

DAY 18

THE SHOUT

> REV 14:6-7 MSG
> *I saw another Angel soaring in Middle-Heaven. He had an Eternal Message to preach to all who were still on earth, every nation and tribe, every tongue and people. He preached in a loud voice, "Fear God and give him glory! His hour of judgment has come! Worship the Maker of Heaven and earth, salt sea and fresh water!"*

This angel is flying at the highest point in the sky, shouting with the loudest voice to reach the maximum amount of people. His message is urgent as this is God's last appeal to a world filled with people He desperately loves. The message he heralds is not only the gospel, it's the eternal everlasting gospel. This good news has always been and will never change that God loves the world from the foundation. It is multi-national, non-racial, and a message for every people group on the earth. The appeal is for us to revere God and give Him adoration. There is also hope for the nations because God's judgment has arrived. In Acts 8:33 Jesus is denied this same judgment that He now gets to offer. Governments, lawmakers, and courts all fall short of offering the nations justice. Jesus is the only just judge who can offer true justice to the earth. The hour of Christ's justice has come. He has a right to judge the earth because He created it (Col 1:16). We are in the hour now, these are the last days. Have you noticed how much more Christians are becoming aware of the biblical mandate for social justice? There is an awakening taking place as we all unite with this angel and cry for justice. What is your cry?

Today's Prayer

Lord, allow me to sound the cry of Justice in my own neighborhood. Give me the voice I need to call out injustice and to stand with those who need Your support. Direct my path as I travel from home to work, to school, to church, let the cry be heard through my actions. Let those who interact with me trust that I have their best interests at heart and are willing to rely on my support in serving them. Help me to realize that I am not alone on this journey. Point me to people who are crying out with the angel and let our cry be heard this week.
Amen.

My Reflections

DAY 19

DIVISION VS UNITY

Rev 21:1-4 NASB
Then I saw a new heaven and a new earth; for the first heaven and the first earth passed away, and there is no longer any sea. And I saw the holy city, new Jerusalem, coming down out of heaven from God, made ready as a bride adorned for her husband. And I heard a loud voice from the throne, saying, "Behold, the tabernacle of God is among men, and He will dwell among them, and they shall be His people, and God Himself will be among them, and He will wipe away every tear from their eyes; and there will no longer be any death; there will no longer be any mourning, or crying, or pain; the first things have passed away."

The part of this passage that always fascinates me is when John looks and notices that there is "no longer any sea". Growing up I had the unique privilege of traveling across the world at a young age. Our high school took us to London, Spain, France, and even Morocco! It was an epic experience that opened my eyes to the vastness of our world. It helped me to broaden my worldview and consider life outside of America. In many ways I believe traveling helps people become less prejudiced and more open to other ways of thinking. Unfortunately, in some countries, especially America, people never travel across the sea. After the great flood as recorded in the Bible, the world typography changed significantly allowing large bodies of water to divide the land. The tower of babel showdown confirmed the separation of people by nations, tribes, and tongues. It seems God divides the earth to keep sinful people from uniting again for catastrophic global evil. With modern technology (i.e. the internet) it seems the world is quickly coming back together again. Some fear a new world order, migrant takeover, or moral degradation. There is a fear with the nations coming back together as we see happening in America. The beauty of what John sees is that God does seek to bring the world together again. Part of what we see happening is an opportunity for us to reach the world for Jesus and prepare them for His return. Missionary work is easier today as the nation's come to us. As we interact with other cultures and people, we are foreshadowing the day when there will be no more separation between the people of God.

Today's Prayer

Lord, it's hard to walk in this world and not feel alone because we tend to be about our own business. Help me to stop and notice the people around me. Give me a mind of unity and community. Help me seek out those in my community who need You. Let them see You in me, and allow them to be open to my actions. As I let go of my judgmental ways, help those who I am interacting with also let go of their own judgements they may have about me. It's not easy, but allow it to be easier each day.
Amen.

My Reflections

DAY 20

GOD WITH US

Rev 21:1-4 NASB
Then I saw a new heaven and a new earth; for the first heaven and the first earth had passed away, and there is no longer any sea. And I saw the holy city, new Jerusalem, coming down out of heaven from God, made ready as a bride adorned for her husband. And I heard a loud voice from the throne, saying, "Behold, the tabernacle of God is among men, and He will dwell among them, and they shall be His people, and God Himself will be among them, and He will wipe away every tear from their eyes; and there will no longer be any death; there will no longer be any mourning, or crying, or pain; the first things have passed away."

While I love traveling and being on vacation, even the best experience can be sad if I am alone. And in the most boring of circumstances can be the best of times if my husband is with me. We recently had to cancel a much-anticipated trip to Dubai and subsequently had to settle with a trip to nearby Atlanta. I know, no comparison, right? While the place was not what we had hoped, we still had an amazing time because we were together. The climax of heaven and what makes heaven, heaven is the permanence of the Emmanuel hope, God with us. Jesus, through the incarnation, gave humanity a taste of this experience. The hope is that Christ will dwell with us. As believers we know the mystery of God which Christ in us is, the very hope of glory (Paul). We are the tabernacle of God in which His Spirit seeks to daily dwell. When we are continually allowing Christ to dwell in us, we prepare for His physical dwelling among us. This passage points us to a wholistic hope for mankind. God fills our spiritual need by promising to dwell with us in a real and tangible way. God fills our emotional pain as He wipes away our tears. God fills our physical need for safety and sustainment by giving us eternal life. Revelation 7:13 adds to this by saying "we will hunger and thirst no more". The social fears and injustices that are realities now will not be present in the earth made new. Can you imagine a life without mourning the loss of a friend or loved one? Can you imagine waking up with no pain? This life is possible and available to those who believe. Sin seeks to block us from envisioning this day. The enemy wants to keep us locked in despair, but it is when we reflect on this coming reality that we unlock our Hope. By elevating our minds, we elevate our spirits. Begin to dwell on the hope of Him dwelling. The hope for a dying world is a living Savior who died for us and will one day live with us.

Today's Prayer

Lord, I know I am nothing without You. As I need You, I know there are others out there that are in need of You. Help me draw those around me to You, through the service of giving my time, energy, and talents. Place in me the burden to bring peace to those who are troubled, place in me the burden to bring support to those who may be alone. As I bring these things, allow Your people to accept You and give themselves to You. Amen.

My Reflections

DAY 21
PRIVILEGED PERSPECTIVES

EZEKIEL 16:49 NASB
Behold, this was the guilt of your sister Sodom: she and her daughters had arrogance, abundant food and careless ease, but she did not help the poor and needy.

Wait! Read that passage again. This is the same Sodom that God destroyed by fire back in Genesis. You read it right, God destroyed an entire city because of their injustice. This reminds us of God's great attention to how we are treating those around us. There are some nations today that would meet the prerequisites for God's just destruction. We see too much corruption and evil done by corporations, governments, authorities and courts. Our complacency makes this type of behavior possible. Too often we have painted the narrative for Sodom and Gomorrah's sin as being evil because of the immorality of each person. Most notably is the idea that they were destroyed because of homosexuality. This however is our own belief of elevating personal piety over public pity. Personal piety deals with our individual responsibility to live moral lives before God. Often these sins are demonized and condemned in a vacuum outside of public pity. Public pity is how we treat and relate to the world around us. The secret is that these two exist in tandem. What we do privately has effects on how we treat those around us publicly. Even if you marooned yourself on an island to keep your personal actions from affecting anyone else, your absence from society still would leave a void. In society you are not only guilty if you are responsible for an injustice but also your inaction makes you complicit with injustice. Think about it, most of what we do personally affects others publicly. When I read the sins of Sodom again, I am rebuked to realize that these failings sound a lot like those of us in America or any other colonized country. It was their privilege that helped them ignore the least fortunate. I wonder if we have made Sodom and Gomorrah such the example of pure evil that we have missed how similar our society has become. While we are pushing for laws to curtail abortion, gay marriage, and immigration, may we remember that Sodom was destroyed because of how she treated the least fortunate, the very ones our "moral" based laws often disenfranchise.

The other day I was meeting with a local Pastor at Starbucks. We were talking about a litany of topics when somehow, we began discussing the LGBTQ+ community. While two Black Pastors were discussing, a white gentleman near us had been listening in and couldn't help but interrupt us to add his two cents. He explained how wrong we were because in his opinion gay relationships are an abomination. Besides inserting himself into our private conversation he totally missed the context of our conversation. In his mind this subject was so cut and dry, so I decided to take the opportunity to give him another perspective. He ironically quoted the common phrase about God destroying Sodom which proves God's distaste against homosexuals. I asked him how he gathered that assumption from the above text. Why would he not focus on the list of social inequitable reasons God said he destroyed Sodom and Gomorrah. He had nothing to say and had to admit he had never read that verse. His theology, like many others has been developed by what others have fed them. We often focus on demonizing individuals, so we feel better about ourselves and ignore our failings to society. Where are some blind spots in your Christian perspective? How can you learn to read the Bible wearing justice lenses? What are some injustices you and your church can speak out against?

Today's Prayer

I understand my privileges as a Christian Lord, and I no longer want to hide behind it. Help me realize my complacency and give me the opportunity to pay attention to the less fortunate. I am asking that You bring to light the things I am blind to, and let me not stand by idly as those less fortunate than I are suffering.
Amen.

My Reflections

DAY 22

ON THE SIDE OF JUSTICE

Rev 14:6-7 MSG
I saw another Angel soaring in Middle-Heaven. He had an Eternal Message to preach to all who were still on earth, every nation and tribe, every tongue and people. He preached in a loud voice, "Fear God and give him glory! His hour of judgment has come! Worship the Maker of Heaven and earth, salt sea and fresh water!"

To many people, judgment seems to be a scary event. We often tell people not to judge us. We want to be free to do what we want without regulation. However, for many living around the world we often lack freedom and fair judgment. Jemel Roberson, Bothom Shem Jean, Jonathan Ferrell, Eric Garner, Laquan McDonald, and so many others all wanted fair judgment, freedom, and due process. These are those who were shot dead, many believe, without due cause by police. The cries of their mothers and fathers are etched in our hearts. The chants from united crowds of activists filling the streets in cities across the country are seared into our minds. The blood of those murdered black bodies stained on the essence of our souls. Those slain were denied their right to due process under the law. The police officer became their judge, jury, and executioner. The blood of the fallen cries out to God for justice. The courts often fail to grant justice or facilitate restoration. To those desperate for justice and often denied their day in court, the judgment of God is a beacon of hope. With Jesus as our judge we can be assured that if judgment has come, this means justice has come. This hour is now. We know this by the prophecy of Daniel that the hour of investigation and judgment has started in heaven. This can only mean one thing; the judge will throw down the gavel soon. The

Bible tells us that Jesus is coming soon and His reward is with Him. He has a reward of eternal life for one group and eternal damnation for another. The hope is that all things will be made right very soon. I want to be on the side of justice; what about you?

Today's Prayer

Lord, as I continue to strengthen my faith in You and realize that You are a Just God, help me not stand on the side of injustice, but to stand with You for Justice. Help me to not just "scroll" on when things happen in our world, but help me to ask questions and get out there and do something. Develop a pain within me that You have for Your creation. Help me show those who are hurt by the injustice of the world to see that You, the God of justice, will deliver Justice. So, I pray that You will help me to counsel, encourage, lift spirits, and be a guide for those who are suffering in pain.
Amen.

My Reflections

DAY 23

WE IN THIS TOGETHER

Amos 8:4-8 NASB
*Listen to this, you who walk all over the weak,
you who treat poor people as less than nothing,
Who say, "When's my next paycheck coming
so I can go out and live it up?
How long till the weekend,
when I can go out and have a good time?"
Who give little and take much,
and never do an honest day's work.
You exploit the poor, using them—
and then, when they're used up, you discard them.
God swears against the arrogance of Jacob:
"I'm keeping track of their every last sin."
God's oath will shake earth's foundations,
dissolve the whole world into tears.
God's oath will sweep in like a river that rises,
flooding houses and lands,
And then recedes,
leaving behind a sea of mud.*

"Imma do me!" is a phrase too often used when a person chooses to disregard others for their own personal pleasure. In many ways American culture has fostered such behavior which celebrates the achievements of the strong. Capitalism has detrimentally affected how we think and how communities live and love together. We must remember that who we are and what we do does affect others. When humanity begins to draw nourishment from its roots, we are reminded of African philosophy of ubuntu which means "humanity" or the idea that "I am because we are". The story goes of an anthropologist studying a tribe in Africa, who sets a bowl of candy under a tree. He drew a line in the dirt and told the children to race towards the bowl. To his surprise the children immediately joined hands, laughing, they ran towards the candy bowl together. Go to any birthday party in America and see what happens when the pinata drops its candy. But to the young African children this was part of their culture, for how could one enjoy the candy when the others had none? This justice ideal was placed into the birthplace of civilizations by our Creator Jesus. We want freedom to do as we please in this life but freedom without the law of love is irresponsible. It angers God when His children act outside of His character. His law of love governs the universe so our actions will not harm ourselves or others. In fact, our actions should help connect us to each other and to God.

Today's Prayer

Father help us to be a community of people who love and care for one another, starting with me. Help me realize that whatever I do is not just for me, but it is for the benefit of others. Develop in me thoughts for my brothers and sisters. Allow me to do nothing without first going to You and asking how what I want to do will help my community. I want to be community-minded. Help me to be community-minded today.
Amen.

My Reflections

DAY 24
FINDING MY RELIGION

JAMES 1:27 NASB
"Pure and undefiled religion in the sight of our God and Father is this: to visit orphans and widows in their distress, and to keep oneself unstained by the world."

Religion today gets a bad rap, and basically anything else related to rules. However, according to this text, religion in its purest and untainted form reaches beyond us and touches those in need. Our religion informs our behavior, it disciplines our lives in accordance with God's will. When we are truly religious, we are impervious to the evil influence of the world. Some years back the mogul songwriter and choir director Kirk Franklin interviewed on WLIB 1190 radio show speaking about his album, Losing my religion. He argued for relationship over religion. He described religion as someone standing on the shore giving instructions to someone drowning instead of jumping in and saving them like Jesus does. While I agree this is how religion has been exercised in many churches, it is not the ideal. We cannot throw away words like religion simply because people in churches have interposed vain tradition upon it. True religion should keep us in relationship or keep us from falling back into the ocean of sin once we have been saved. Often terms like religion, law, and judgment have been demonized by progressives and misused by conservatives. These terms are actually all extremely necessary when reflecting on a life of love. Religion keeps us away from acting on injustice, while the law gives us parameters to protect us from harming ourselves and others, and judgment sets right the wrong that has been committed. It is popular today to dismiss biblical rules and regulations, especially those in the

Old Testament that don't fit into our lifestyle. We claim they have been eradicated, while not understanding the root and purpose of them. Christ fulfilling the law as an example for us, not as an excuse for lawlessness. When we conform our religion to God's love, we become the people He envisioned us to be.

Today's Prayer

As I contemplate on our relationship Lord, please help me not to miss the need of helping others because of vain traditions. If whatever I am doing in the name of religion, or being a "Christian" is getting in the way of genuinely helping one of the least, please remove it from my life and open up my eyes to it. I want to be fully engaged in following You wholeheartedly as You did while on earth. Help me mirror Your life on earth. Allow me to speak up against those who put tradition in place of religion.
Amen.

My Reflections

DAY 25

YOU BECOME WHAT YOU WORSHIP

PSALM 115:1-8 KJV
"Not unto us, O Lord, not unto us, But to Your name give glory, because of Your mercy, Because of Your truth. Why should the Gentiles say, "So where is their God?' But our God is in heaven; He does whatever He pleases. Their idols are silver and gold, the work of men's hands. They have mouths, but they do not speak; eyes they have, but they do not see; they have ears, but they do not hear; noses they have, but they do not smell; they have hands, but they do not handle; feet they have, but they do not walk; nor do they mutter though their throat. Those who make them are like them; so is everyone who trusts them."

I have a few friends who question why social justice is an imperative for their lives. One friend said, "I need to make sure I'm saved first and then I can worry about others". Another friend shared they had no time to do activism or to protest. And even another expressed that Jesus did not protest and that we just have to endure sufferings. These are often the sentiments of the traditional church goers I have encountered. We often feel that prayer, bible study, and worship are personal disciplines for personal growth. While acts of charity and social justice are good practices, they are not essential for salvation. While it is important to have personal time with God, we must remember why we strive to grow personally. We are not living on an Island to ourselves. When we reflect on the issue of idolatry we can often slap on our ultra-legalistic hat and regulate every behavior that we believe is connected to paganism. However, idolatry is more focused on the root not the fruit. Many of us have made our doctrines or denomination an idol.

It is easy to tell who someone idolizes by their behavior.

Some of us think we follow Jesus when we are actually just a fan. You become like what you worship. It is easy to distinguish pharisee's from Jesus.

Jesus went aside to pray and gained power for those he encountered during the day. The entire act of the incarnation and His death on the cross is the greatest protest against oppression. Many activists march forward unyielding in their beliefs and cries for peace, willing to go to jail and even die if need be. Jesus is the forerunner of the so-called social justice warrior. He condescends to our level, dwells with us, relates to us, stands up to the authorities, the oppressors, and died a martyr's death. Are you an idolizer, fan or follower of Christ? How far are you willing to go?

Today's Prayer

Father, I want to be sure that when I am following You, I can go the length. Point out the reason why I am doing the things I do in the name of You. Help me recognize my purpose on this earth and that a part of my purpose is to be of help to others. Although, it can be hard to deal with people, give me the strength this week and every day to know how to deal with all types of people.
Amen.

My Reflections

DAY 26
TAP INTO THE POWER

NEHEMIAH 5:11-12
"'Restore now to them, even this day, their lands, their vineyards, their olive groves, and their houses, also a hundredth of the money and the grain, the new wine and the oil, that you have charged them.' So they said, 'We will restore it, and will require nothing from them; we will do as you say,'"

*L*et us just say this up front; Nehemiah was that dude! Nehemiah has the biblical reputation of an activist who got things done. Just take some time and study the entire book, it is quite inspiring. In chapter 5 Nehemiah sought to resolve a major problem of exploitation against the people in the city. It had gotten so bad that people were going into debt and selling their lands just to eat and survive. The oppressors were forcing their children into slavery and trafficking their daughters. Nehemiah's reaction was pure anger and he demanded immediate action and restoration from the oppressors. His courage and boldness saved the lives of the people in that city.

In the city my wife and I are currently ministering in, there is an outcry for food. Many grocery stores have closed down with liquor stores often taking their place. Some of the concerned citizens couldn't take it anymore and got together to protest the detestable actions of owners and inaction of city officials. We had a small group that supported the movement and also wanted to seek sustainable solutions for the food desert crisis. We prayed and money began to flow for the funding of the Hope Garden, a community garden planted in the midst of an impoverished neighborhood. We plan to educate, feed, and revive our community by addressing these problems with justice-centered solutions. The fight is far from done, we are just getting started but the story of Nehemiah gives us fuel to move forward. What is your fuel? What is stopping you today to stand up and shout?

Today's Prayer

Father, I know there is much around me that needs to be done, but I do not know where to start. I am asking that You invigorate me and show me where to begin. Like Nehemiah, help me to stand with others to fight against the issues that are plaguing my community. Help me rally a group of people, or join a group that is already developed to fight the injustice. I know You have not given me a spirit of fear, but of power and a sound mind. Help me tap into this today.
Amen.

My Reflections

DAY 27
SPIRIT ACTION

Nehemiah 1:3-4, NKJV
"And they said to me, "The survivors who are left from the captivity in the province are there in great distress and reproach. The wall of Jerusalem is also broken down, and its gates are burned with fire. So it was, when I heard these words, that I sat down and wept, and mourned for many days; I was fasting and praying before the God of heaven."

We recently preached a sermon series in our church on this book. The series was titled "Reviving the City". We spoke much on the power of personal and community revival. As the church is revived so will the city be revived. Nehemiah teaches us how to use prayer, strategy, and boldness to turn around an entire city. Yes, sometimes his anger seemed a little unbridled, i.e. 13:25 but hey he used his passion for God and got results. Sometimes seeking justice requires some radical action for there to be results. It is the foundation that the book begins with that is key for any movement. Prayer must be at the forefront of every movement towards change. Nehemiah had a powerful prayer life. Prayer is essential in this battle because one can easily drift off towards their own desires and agenda. Prayer reminds us that this fight is not ours it belongs to God. Prayer also fills us with the Holy Spirit and leads us to make the next move. In my life, praying while seeking justice has saved me so much time. Instead of getting frustrated and overwhelmed I am learning to look for the opportunities God is opening for my gifts.

Recently our city has been plagued with gun violence and many have lost their lives. Across the nation in America, gun violence has been a heated topic of discussion with very little change in policy. For those who seek bi-partisan solutions the appeal for prayer can seem counter- productive. Not that prayer is not important, but rather that action is now required. I believe that true and lasting action comes as a direct result of prayer. My friend and I went to see the wife of one of the victims of the violence. As we walked into her house, we could feel the pain and tension in the room. My friend reached for the young widow and held her as she released her pain sobbing in this strangers' arms. The release became contagious and other family members began to feel the Spirit in the room healing their hurt. Outside the house three or four boys sat unmoved by the emotional breakthrough happening just feet away. I went out to them as the spiritual warfare was visible; they were contemplating revenge. The Spirit spoke through me and their demeanor began to shift. Before they knew it, they were in the house with us as we all joined hands and cried out to God. We had come simply to pray with them, but God used that experience to possibly divert a revenge shooting. Just the pure empathy of strangers entering their home to pray broke the chains and banished the demon of revenge. Allow prayer to move you to action. Reflect on the issues in your community that first need your prayer and the Spirit's action.

Today's Prayer

Lord, our community has been riddled with _____ and _____. I am asking that You take these concerns and change it for the better. Our community is in need of _____ and _____. Help me to discover what I can do to help, and lead me to others who want to help as well. Give me some ideas to reach out in whatever capacity is needed to bring some relief. Amen.

My Reflections

DAY 28

GOLDEN RULE

Exodus 22:21
"Do not mistreat an alien or oppress him, for you were aliens in Egypt."

When you have experienced injustice, you should know how to treat those who are being mistreated. I should never forget where I come from. Many of us, if not most, can trace our history to some humble beginnings. We were not born into a lineage with no faults, hardships, or flaws. The one who was born fully God and fully man chose to be born into a tainted lineage. Jesus claims the lineage of bondage even though He is God. He came to dwell among those who needed Him, to receive those who were mistreated and oppressed. We are often reminded in scriptures that we are recipients of grace, it is nothing of ourselves that we should boast about our pedigree.

Jesus told a parable about the servant owing a King several million dollars and is forgiven this debt while he is unable to forgive his brother who owes him a few dollars. The parable highlights the ridiculous hypocrisy of being the recipient of grace but not granting this gift to others. The text is speaking specifically to how citizens of a country treat immigrants. There is a moral and religious responsibility to protect and treat with dignity persons migrating or seeking refuge in your country. All except Native and Black Americans migrated to America, which means a vast majority of Americans, especially should hear the message of this scripture. We should be careful when aligning ourselves with any political movement, rhetoric, or actions that give the hint of mistreating immigrants. Nationalism has no place in the hearts of

God's people. We are told to welcome with open arms those from other shores or beyond our borders. The reasoning for this is quite simple for God. He wishes for the world to learn of Him, what better way than bringing them from around the world to your doorstep. We treat people the way we would have wanted to be treated.

Today's Prayer

As I reflect on the mistreatment of those around me, I pray that I am not taking part in any conversations, or actions that are affecting the wellbeing of others. Lord, direct my thoughts and actions to mirror what You would do if you were on this Earth right now. Use me to help, rather than be a burden or hindrance in the life of those who have migrated to our country.
Amen.

My Reflections

DAY 29

THE PARADIGM SHIFT

> JONAH 4:10-11, KJV
> *"Then said the Lord, Thou hast had pity on the gourd, for which thou hast not laboured, neither madest it grow; which came up in a night, and perished in a night: And should not I spare Nineveh, that great city, wherein are more than sixscore thousand persons that cannot discern between their right hand and their left hand; and also much cattle?"*

Some of the most contentious conflicts I have experienced have involved church people having pointless arguments. People will have a fit to protect their sacred tradition, have their way, or to be proved right. Many times, they are so blinded by their own desires and comforts they don't see how divisive their opinions are to the church. On a trip to speak to a group of Pastors in Idaho, my friend took me to eat with a young Pastor and his family. We sat and ate while talking about his ministry experience. He started preaching out of his house five years ago with his wife and two kids, then the ministry grew to 500 people. They renovated an old grocery store into a place of worship. As soon as I walked into the facility, I knew it was something special. They were intentional about every aspect, even the smell of the lobby. He talked about the dead set focus the entire church shares for advancing God's kingdom. They recognize they exist to reach out to others. They are there for the least, the last, and the lost. But they don't just talk about it, they exemplify it even in where they park their cars on Sunday morning. The pastor described seeing an elderly woman walking across the street to get to the building. The peculiar thing was that she bypassed some prime parking spaces directly in front of the church building. Why wouldn't she park there? Well she's a member and she is already saved. "So what?" You say? If you're like me, you know church folk who you dare not even look at their sacred parking space or their pew for that matter. But this woman and all the members of this church know that the best parking spaces were for new believers and guests. They chose to be uncomfortable so that the lost could easily access Jesus' church.

In our above verse Jonah is complaining about the discomfort of losing a plant God gave Him for shade. In Jonah's anger toward losing a commodity he was not entitled to, revealed his mindset of privilege. God rebukes Him and reminds Jonah of the value of human beings which God loves and wants to save. When we drive past neighborhoods to get to a building may we open our eyes to the people who need us to be their church. May our own preferences and obsession with "doing church" never keep us from truly being the church in our community. May our hearts ache for people like Christ's heart aches. May we care about the people and even the animals above our own comfort.

Today's Prayer

Father open my eyes as I drive to see who I am passing on my way to church. Let me see the neighborhoods and the people like never before. Create a yearning to reach out, rather than pass by. Help me be the church that worships You by doing, helping, spending time, and seeking out the least, last, and lost. Amen.

My Reflections

DAY 30

LAST WORD

MAL 3:5 MSG
"Yes, I'm on my way to visit you with Judgment. I'll present compelling evidence against sorcerers, adulterers, liars, those who exploit workers, those who take advantage of widows and orphans, those who are inhospitable to the homeless – anyone and everyone who doesn't honor me."

At the beginning of this chapter we are reminded of our duty as forerunners like John the Baptist to prepare the way for Christ to return. The Messiah, the King, our Savior is coming back, and He is coming back with a purpose. He has entrusted our salvation out of this sinful world into His hands. He puts us through the fire so like silver, we may be refined as the dross falls away. The master knows the silver is refined when he can see his reflection in the metal. Our sin is what causes injustice and he wants to purge us of the oppressor's influence. We are to reflect the character of Jesus and prepare the way for others to hope in the coming justice. When we live our lives for justice and love we prepare the way for Jesus to return. As the verse explains, His coming will bring about judgement and justice against workers of exploitation and injustice. The good news of Revelation 14 is that the "hour of His judgment" is come. We often fear judgement, but judgment is nothing for a Christian to fear. The final judgment of God justifies the righteous and vindicates the character of God. The great hope is that if judgment has come then justice has also come. When we think about Tamir Rice, Philando Castile, Eric Garner and so many others we ache for because they were robbed of their day in court. Their murderers did not receive the judgment based on the laws of the land. But we can rest assured that the God who knows all and sees all will fix it all. If those impeding justice never repent, they will face the righteous justice of God. In the moment it hurts, and it looks bleak. The fight against injustice is long and tedious. We often feel like change moves at a snail's pace. But as we continue the good fight, we are partnering with the heart of God. We are calling people to hope in the One who will restore all things and repair what has been broken. We hope in our God, the God of justice. To those feeling lost and despondent remember that the laws and leaders of this land are subjected to the King of the Universe, He will have the last word.

Today's Prayer

Lord, I have comfort in knowing that You are a just God that will bring Justice when You return. I want to be a part of the movement that restores sons to their mothers, daughters to their fathers, and wipes the tears from the eyes who have suffered for too long. Help me be a part of Your movement today by fulfilling Your calling on my life to help others. Amen.

My Reflections

DAY 31
TO KNOW HIM

JEREMIAH 22:14-16 NASB
*Who says, 'I will build myself a roomy house
With spacious upper rooms,
And cut out its windows,
Paneling it with cedar and painting it bright red.'
"Do you become a king because you are competing in cedar? Did not your father eat and drink
And do justice and righteousness?
Then it was well with him.
"He pled the cause of the afflicted and needy;
Then it was well.
Is not that what it means to know Me?"
Declares the Lord.*

To know God is to know justice. What do people know about us? Are we known for how we plead for the cause of the afflicted and needy? A true King is not measured by how much power and money they have but by how they give. The King of Kings teaches us to look outward before seeking selfish pleasures. Our task is to seek first the kingdom of God and His righteousness (Matt 6:33). In other words, the very first of our desires should be the rulership of God and doing His justice. We have no right to have selfish desires when following after God. It is God who teaches us to seek and save the lost. It is Jesus who shows us the model of healing and touching the poor. It is Jesus who shows us a custom of liberation and prayer. It is Jesus who shows us the character of God. For God so loved the world that He gave. Yes, God loved so it led Him to give. This is the direct action of love. Love explains El as Elohim; the living God our Yahweh, El Shaddai; the Almighty God, El elyon; the most-high God, El roi; the God who sees me, El Olam; the everlasting God. Love gave His only begotten son. Love gives from its only, from a place of value and endearment. Love creates so that it can fulfill. Love desires to save, whomever, simply has belief in love.

Our prayer is that you have discovered the God of love during this 31-devotional journey. May His love fill your heart and lead you to give like He gives. May we seek to offer people Jesus. May we be so consumed with His Spirit that when people encounter us, they encounter God. May the type of actions we do for our world reflect the type of God we worship. May our actions speak louder than our words. Our life is a book that people we may never know get to read. Our greatest prayer is that when people from all walks of life, no matter their gender, orientation, melanin saturation, religion, or political affiliation, when they read your book may they read the book of El.

Today's Prayer

Lord, may I be consumed with your Love.
Amen.

My Reflections

APPENDIX

EXPLORING UBUNTU AND RESTORATIVE JUSTICE

BY JOSHUA NELSON, DMin

Topics of restorative, social, or distributive justice have become charged political terms in recent years. When discussing the topic of restorative justice in society, it would be prudent to learn the implications being prescribed.

The term "justice" is important to define as various cultures view it differently. For western thinkers the idea of justice deals primarily with balance. The image of lady justice is often the depiction of the western understanding of justice. Lady justice stands tall with a sword in one hand, a balancing scale in the other, and she is blindfolded. This image originating from Greek thought and perfected by Roman governance speaks to the blind fairness and exactness by which justice should rightly be administered. The issue Marshall (2015), has with such an emblem is that justice is primarily concerned only with facts and the ability to balance the rule of law.

Levad (2016) suggests that "justice" used in the restorative sense seeks to "repair harm" rather than focus on the punitive nature of justice as has been the recent results of criminal justice. Marshall goes as far to suggest that restorative justice sometimes requires bias rather than balance. As Evans (2015) reveals, justice should be lopsided towards the mistreated, the victim. Moreover, when speaking about restorative justice the goal is less about balancing the scales or "getting even" but more about the rehabilitation and reconciliation between victim and offender. This means that the scale is lost all together and wholeness becomes the primary focus for all parties involved.

The parties most concerned within restorative justice include the a) community members affected by the incident, the b) family members directly affected, and quite naturally the c) victim(s) and the offender(s) (Zehr, 2010; Ashworth, 2002; Brazemore, 1999). With this understanding justice becomes more of an ideal or a quest for peace in the community. A society that practices restorative justice would not question whether "justice was served" but rather if "justice was offered" toward the entire community affected by the offense.

It is imperative to note the complexity of understanding restorative justice practices. This term has been used fluidly in association with criminal justice and in many cases misused. While primarily a method for criminal justice reform, the International Institute for Restorative Practices are helping apply restorative justice principles in schools, churches, and in various levels of business.

Western origins of restorative justice can be linked to the Mennonites of 1974 or through the work of Albert Arthur Eglash coining the phrase in his 1977 article "Beyond Restitution: Creative restitution". But the concept of restorative justice can be traced to Africa, where civilization began, and can be found within one African conglomerated word, ubuntu (Omale, 2006). This word, a composite of various African languages means "wholeness of personhood" or as Van Ness and Strong (2002) best put it, "I am because you are, or my humanity is tied with your humanity". This concept is what modern restorative practices seek to create, a community of wholeness. Thus restoration seeks to create repair, rehabilitation, or wholeness.

Some, like Llewellyn and Howse (2002) argue that at

the core of both western and non-western culture is a restorative model of justice and thus restorative justice is not a "new-age justice" but rather a, returning to our roots.

There is record of ancient societies using restorative principles such as family group conferences and circle hearings, demonstrated with the Aboriginals, the Inuit, and natives of North and South America. Weitekamp (2003) found it ironic that after the year 2000 there was revitalized interest in returning to restorative practices that had been used "some millennia ago by our ancestors" (p. 111). Many historians note that colonialism had a major part to play in these systems of restorative justice being dismantled. In New Zealand, pre-Norman Ireland, and in Pacific nations like Tonga, Fiji, and Samoa, restorative justice was also incorporated within their culture (Consedine, 1999).

While other ingenious cultures share a history of restorative principles the practice of state led justice or retributive justice emerges as a direct result of colonialism. Post and pre-colonial Africa are in stark contrast. According to Zehr (1999) a revolution began in the eleventh or twelfth centuries moving the west away from restorative justice practices towards a state centered form of justice. This resulted in what Zehr calls the "reconceptualization of the nature of disputes" which left the state as the keepers of the peace. Now if an offender violated the law the state was considered the victim. This brand of justice denies the holistic approach of umbutu which seeks "holistic justice", not from the point of the judge but the victim and community.

By disallowing the effects of restorative justice, some believe this causes harm to the wholeness and wellbeing of communities. Louw (2006) asserts a positive case for restorative justice because it creates space for venting, expression, and release for victims. And for the offender, Zehr admits that dialogue may not lead to reconciliation of the victim and offender, but by engaging in restorative principles their perception of one another would become better, thus a better community. The offender has an opportunity to see what his harm has caused. At the same time the restorative process can uncover the "why" that many victims often wonder.

African culture was and, in many cases, still is centered on the strong belief of an individual's inseparable connection to their family and community. Because of this, an individual's behavior directly reflects their upbringing. In the case of an offender who must make amends, this responsibility can fall upon the members of their community (Elechi et al., 2010).

Akeredolu (2016) shares much needed information on the intricate postcolonial justice systems in Africa and the community ideal for restoration. Today in small communities, African indigenous justice systems address community concerns and crimes before they reach the state level. Elechi et al. (2010) retells a case that gives a good example of restorative practices and their potential.

"A 25-year-old man who was caught stealing yams from a community member's farm. The defendant admitted to the yam theft allegation leveled against him. He was ordered to return the yams to the owner and also pay a fine to the community for theft. He returned the yams to the owner and apologized to him and to the community for his bad behavior. However, he said he had no means of paying the fine that the village tribunal imposed on him. He appealed to the community for their understanding on the grounds that he had no job and had no hope of securing one in the near future. During the community's deliberation, it was learned that the individual in question lost his parents at a very young age; thus, he had no education and transferable skills he could use to secure a job. The tribunal members decided that the defendant's uncle, who they believed had sufficient resources to send the young man to school or assist him in learning a trade he could use in securing a job, should be held responsible for the young man's fine. The defendant's uncle under the threat of a hefty fine was also ordered to assist the defendant to either attend school or learn a trade. Appeal was also made to other community members to assist in finding a job for the young man."

"Restorative justice principles and practices have the potential to deliver a better kind of justice than what exists currently. With respect to racial-ethnic and cultural differences, the potential exists in the openness of the process to differing cultural sensibilities and to addressing relations of inequality. It has the potential to promote a "dialogic view of morality" compared to a "monologic voice of law." It can make the justice system process more humane. But that potential cannot be assumed in the abstract or by passing a new law. This conversation needs to be part of a broader engagement with the politics of race, class, and culture (Daly, 2000).

For more information and resources on restorative justice please visit www.restorativejustice.org, www.NACRJ.org, and watch the Redemption Project on CNN by Van Jones.

CHARITY VS. JUSTICE SPECTRUM

Gift a Fish – providing free basic needs or resources
Teach to Fish – implementing training, education, mentors, knowledge
Tools to Fish – connecting to essential resources, networking, agencies
Pond to Fish – unlocking access to opportunities, filling voids, effective legislation
Fish in Pond – viability and sustainability of opportunities, economy
Quality of Fish – equality and equity in resources, goods, and services
Life of Pond – assuring multiple streams of sustainability and revenue
Market Fish – assuring longevity, assuring unique niche, generational education
Own the Pond – becoming in full control of ones' own destiny and resources
Beyond Fish – opening additional areas of ownership and expandability, ability to provide for others and cycle back for holistic sustainability.

ACTIONS OF LOVE

PRACTICAL STEPS TOWARDS A LIFE OF LOVE AND JUSTICE

- Educate yourself on local concerns
- Interact with neighbors and people who live and work in your community
- Attend city council meetings and get to know local officials
- Attend and participate in community ran meetings
- Advocate for legislation
- Start projects that address the concerns in your community. Remember to involve those you intend to serve.
- Call your local congressperson and share your opinions
- Read candidates profiles and websites, attend townhall meetings and ask questions
- Run for office yourself
- Engage in peaceful demonstrations
- Use social media to engage on important topics
- Conduct local surveys and seek to address concerns with a group of people
- Raise money for projects, apply for grants, crowdfunding
- Conduct one-on-one meetings with influential people or write letters to organizations and companies for support
- Get involved with community service
- Get to know your local reporters and share important stories.

SOCIAL JUSTICE PROJECT IDEAS

- Plant a community garden to address health and food deserts
- Build affordable housing
- Challenge slum lords and improve living conditions
- Speak out against any unequal treatment by the city towards certain low-income neighborhoods
- Develop community watches and partner with local police to hold events for young people to get to know police
- Start an enditnow© campaign to deter domestic violence
- Provide a transportation service for low-income who need to go to work but can't afford public transportation; or look into the city providing vouchers
- Collaborate with local judges and city to connect people who have received misdemeanors to jobs and other resources
- Create a local business league for Black or minority businesses
- Develop a support group for victims of gun violence
- Organize advocates for incarcerated and their families
- Collect a list of all local resources and non-profits and give to people who need to be made aware
- Educate and teach health principles
- Provide for immigrants at the southern border
- After school tutoring
- Free Wi-Fi hotspots
- Victim support for families who have lost loved ones to gun violence.

BIBLIOGRAPHY

Akeredolu, O. (2016). *The Indigenous African Criminal Justice System for the Modern World.* Durham, NC: Carolina Academic Press.

Ashworth, A. (2002). Responsibilities, Rights and Restorative Justice. *British Journal of Criminology*, 43(3), 578-595.

Bazemore, G. (1999). The fork in the road to juvenile court reform. *Annals of the American Academy of Political and Social Science*, 564, 81-108.

Consedine, J. (1999). *Restorative Justice: Healing the effect of crime*, New Zealand: Ploughshares.

Daly, K. (2000). Restorative Justice in Diverse and Unequal Societies. *Law in Context*, 17(1), 167.

Elechi, O., Morris, S.V.C., & Schauer. E.J. (2010). *Restoring Justice (Ubuntu): An African Perspective.* International Criminal Justice Review, 20(1), 73-85.

Evans, P. (2015). Imagining justice for the marginalized: A suspicious reading of the covenant code (Exod 20:22-23:33) in its Ancient Near Eastern context. In C. Westfall & B. Dyer (Eds.), *The Bible and social justice* (MNTS) (pp. 1-34). Eugene, OR: Wipf & Stock.

Levad, A. (2016). Restorative and transformative justice in a land of mass incarceration. *Journal of Moral Theology*, 5(2), 22-43.

Llewellyn, J.J. and Howse, R. (2002). *Restorative Justice: A conceptual framework*, Canada: Law Commission.

Louw, D. J. (2006). The African concept of Ubuntu and restorative justice. In D. Sullivan & L. Tifft (Eds.), *Handbook of restorative justice: A global perspective* (pp. 151-160). New York: Taylors & Francis Group.

Marshall, C. (2015). *The little book of biblical justice: A fresh approach to the Bible's teachings on justice.* New York, NY: Good Books.

Omale, D.J.O. (2006). Justice in history: an examination of 'African restorative traditions' and the emerging 'restorative justice' paradigm. *African Journal of Criminology & Justice Studies: AJCJS*, 2(2), 33.

Van Ness, D and Strong, K.H. (2002). *Restorative Justice* 2nd ed., Cincinnati, OH: Anderson Publishing.

Weitekamp, E.G.M. (2003). *The History of Restorative Justice. A Restorative Justice Reader,* Oregon USA: Willan publishing: pp.111-124.

Zehr, H. (2015). *The little book of restorative justice.* New York, NY: Good Books.

ABOUT THE AUTHORS

Joshua and Kimberly Nelson are married, and live in southwest Georgia with their two children, their daughter Kaleah Jade and their son Jude King. They lead active ministries in their community through their non-profit Mind Body and Soul Consultation, Incorporated. Their business is centered on serving the holistic needs of individuals and families. They are both devoted followers of Jesus Christ, who believe their faith should be spoken and demonstrated.

Joshua is the Pastor of two churches and oversees an Academy and Daycare. He has been a Pastor since 2007 in North and South Carolina and is hired by the South Atlantic Conference of Seventh-day Adventists. He attended Oakwood University receiving a BBA in management and BA in theology with a minor in biblical languages. He holds a DMin in Urban Ministry from Andrews University. He is the author of In the Trenches: 10 reasons to stay in ministry and former host of the Pure Choices television program on the 3ABN Dare to Dream network. Joshua has written for a number of articles, appeared in multiple news stories, and spoken throughout the country in connection with the subject of restorative and social justice. Joshua has been instrumental in the formation of a community garden project, reorganization of the Albany/Dougherty NAACP branch as the interim President, and the creation and administration of the Faith Integrity and Training Intervention Manual for Police and young Black men. He enjoys traveling with family, hiking, and golfing.

Kimberly Nelson is a professor at Fort Valley State University, an HBCU. She teaches school counselors in the Education department. She attended Long Island University where she received a BA in Psychology and English, she attended Andrews University receiving an MA in school counseling, and finally the University of South Carolina with her Ph.D. in counselor education and supervision. Before teaching, Kimberly worked as a family counselor in Brooklyn, NY and school counselor at Camden High in South Carolina. Kimberly has published various articles, presented at conferences throughout the country, and taught classes at New York University. She has an active Instagram page where she showcases her creative homeschool ideas and hacks. She enjoys traveling with family, knitting, and reading.

www.ingramcontent.com/pod-product-compliance
Lightning Source LLC
Chambersburg PA
CBHW050206130526
44591CB00035B/2293